Mozart's Pigtail

Also by Roderick Townley

Poetry

Final Approach
Three Musicians
Summer Street (chapbook)
Blue Angels Black Angels (chapbook)

Criticism

The Early Poetry of William Carlos Williams
Night Errands: How Poets Use Dreams (editor)

Fiction

Minor Gods (novel)

Nonfiction

Safe and Sound: A Parent's Guide to Child Protection

Translation

Paul and Sebastian

Novels for young readers

The Sylvie Cycle (trilogy):
    The Great Good Thing
    Into the Labyrinth
    The Constellation of Sylvie
Sky
The Red Thread
The Blue Shoe
The Door in the Forest
A Bitter Magic

Mozart's Pigtail

poems

Roderick Townley

BkMk Press
University of Missouri-Kansas City

BkMk Press
University of Missouri-Kansas City
5101 Rockhill Road
Kansas City, MO 64110

Executive Editor: Christie Hodgen
Managing Editor: Ben Furnish
Assistant Managing Editor: Cynthia Beard

Cover photo: Stephen McNally Black and White Landscape photographer based in the UK.
Author photo: Spencer Townley-Lott

Partial support for this project has been provided by the Missouri Arts Council, a state agency.

See page 68 for a complete list of donors to BkMk Press.

Library of Congress Cataloging-in-Publication Data

Names: Townley, Rod, author.
Title: Mozart's pigtail : poems / Roderick Townley.
Description: Kansas City, MO : BkMk Press, [2020] | Summary: "Mozart's
  Pigtail comprises a series of poem portraits of musicians, writers, and
  intimate friends as a way of honoring the meaningful connections in the
  poet's life"-- Provided by publisher.
Identifiers: LCCN 2020012723 | ISBN 9781943491247 (paperback)
Subjects: LCGFT: Poetry.
Classification: LCC PS3570.O93 M69 2020 | DDC 811/.54--dc23
LC record available at https://lccn.loc.gov/2020012723

ISBN: 978-1-943491-24-7

For Wyatt
il miglior fabbro

Contents

I

Pulling Out the Stops

Mozart's Pigtail

I was braiding Mozart's hair,
morning sun

filling the room (Constanze
nowhere to be seen), when

all at once (you won't
believe it) the man

jumps up and makes a run
for the piano. I trot

behind, still holding
his pigtail, mind you, even

when he sits
and starts in. I know some

who'd have taken offense.
Not I. I remember once,

I was doing Frau von H.
I abandoned an elaborate coif

at a whim (I can't call it
anything else), and went

for swirl. She loved it. "You
are an artist!" she cried.

He's the same. In fact,
so lovely a largo

it was that I
let go, although

the braid unwound
and I had to begin again.

A Minor God

Old Hiller, music's *deus minor*, died
cynical and sick, his six grand operas
tepidly received, symphonies, lieder,
oratorios galore, lovely things all.

"One could reproach him," Liszt sniffed, "for not
having faults." Had friends instead. Short,
dark-eyed, round, expressive, he gestured
over pastries at a sidewalk boîte

with Chopin, Mendelssohn, and the rest,
unaware his name would not appear
with theirs. He would be known for those
he knew, and for a thing he'd done on a dare

long ago, age fifteen, frightened, advancing
with scissors on the dead Beethoven
and snipping off a coil of his maddening hair.

The Return

for Clair Leonard

On the organ I'd accompany the sun's
last light among empty pews, or sit,
not playing, listening to the elms list
and sparrows turn into leaves. You knew it,
and knew your fate, and forgave my Buxtehude.

I return to find your grave exultant
with ivy, darkly shining, close to the ground
and nippling the hill with green amid the brown
of an autumn afternoon. Nothing hurried,
nothing by halves, you've turned into the world.

Having come so far, I follow my hunch
down to the chapel, slide onto the bench
and listen. In the corner, a sudden presence:
your old shoes stand where you'd always kept them.
Outside, leaves are turning into sparrows
and elms into ships. I pull out the stops
and play for dear life all the changes I know.

Requiem

for Lennie Tristano

1

         I was going to say
       before the news came
    of your death
something
    about the opening
        lines of a
           woman's legs.

Let them stand
as the opening lines
of your requiem.

      A heart atta, atta
          (I can't read
    obits in *Time*
        those smooth asses
   sessments make
     me stut)

        Started to say
            something
      about the left-handed
    dare of your
descending bass.

    I know the game
    you went down for
    you are better than I
    at tracing the braille
    revelations of jazz

of opening lines
and sex songs.

Blind at nine
you had no choice.

I see you
a skinny kid
at a big piano

oblivious
noodling out a tune

even then cutting in at
an angle.

2

Thought I caught sight of you
within the glass
heartbeat
of a revolving door.

Scribbled a line on the back
of a bill I
can't pay
but you'd already gone.

Getting nervous now—
running to the
airport
to pick up wife and boy.

Haven't seen them in months
so you see
your death
is an inconvenience.

Your life was an inconvenience.
　　　Your music rides
　　　　　rough shod
over people's feelings.

3

It will be cold in Queens.
Here under the eyes of bees
and the corrugated sun
　　　　　of a southern
　　　　　　　bitching continent
earth stinks and steams,

good men gunned down
　　　by the goons of obedience
　　　　　their bodies stuffed in ovens
and their names erased.

　　　　　Yet I hear the chink
　　　of ice
　　picks on frozen ground
tucking you in
　　　and the ticking
　　　　　of a sweating clock

　　halting
　　　hurrying on
　　　　　counting off the days
　　on crooked fingers

and you now missing all ten yours
　　what they could do
　　　your "chops"
　　　　　as you put it in that

jazz punk talk
          you'd sling me
                    between licks.

                    That's how it was
          talking to you
     in 5/4
winter nights in Queens.

4

It hasn't been easy
shadowing you,
in darkness difficult

though I'd hear you
ahead of me and follow
your tracks by feel.

I've had to go the long way around,
using distance
as you used darkness,

as a blind, as a cape
flashing the brief shapes
of continents.

In a shaky hand
I try in buses, boats, planes
for a rough graph

of vectors, tremulous outlines
of a thing
we both are after,

dead or alive.

The Cellist

for Jacqueline du Pré

1

Within the instrument, at a
precise point connecting neck
and back, a block is placed. Three
millimeters off and the tone
is altered. Ten, and an audience
can tell. The French call it *l'âme*,
the soul. But what is it, this soul?
What but precision in a wind-
storm of wood, hair, gut, steel,
sob and bone? To fetch it out, you
hug a body the size of a row-
boat, legs wrapped around it, knees
holding tight, feet planted for balance,
muscles from shoulder to wrist
bowing like mad while the fingers
pound down thick strings
till there's blood on the fingerboard.

*It was my gorgeous secret. It became
a person, even a love.*

Midnight. Outside the glass,
snow flings itself about, a
white-haired maniac. Look out
at its violence, its silence. Here
in this shaken snowglobe
of a house, soundlessness
is a note held and held. Knowing
the intimacy of distance
she played to the balcony,
to me, for instance, this evening

decades ago, despite numbness
in the fingertips, and blurring sight.
It was there already, hidden
from her fans, the shadow
of a wing fluttering
in her long-boned hands.

2

Tomorrow, and snow resumes
like a second movement. The Elgar
sings us through it,
the performance at Kingsway Hall
that made her famous.
Yet when she heard it,
what she'd done there, she burst
into tears: "That was not what I meant!"

To lose precision, to live sans this,
sans that, sans all but sanity—hell
was on her scent. At first, the diagnosis,
what relief! Not crazy after all! It was
simply this body, this "multiple
fuckosis," screwing with her. Soon
coming downstairs meant sliding
down on her bum. Small pleasures
intensified: strong coffee, fine
chocolate, as loss after loss, step
after bumping step, fifteen years of it,
ran her at last to ground. And she

such an early riser! Age five
climbing onto the ironing board
to switch on the wireless—the BBC
introducing the instruments.
Hearing the cello, she called to
her mama: "I want to make that sound!"

Plain blouse and pleated skirt
among the debutantes: "I must go
for a run!" she'd shout, and race off
around the Fenton House gardens.
"Then she'd come back
and we'd play Bach," said her friend.
"With the first stroke of the bow
across the strings . . . you . . . had the feeling,
My God, who's in there?"

3

The great world, pawing
its press releases, lifted its snout
to the wind and sniffed her out, this
golden girl who'd caused Casals
to weep and led an adolescent
Prince Charles to take the cello up.

Moscow, Prague, London, the
Hollywood Bowl. She loved it all,
till she began falling down
and had to wait for someone
to lift her. Beneath the tra-la-la
of gold silk, she wore
a "disgusting" wool vest
to absorb the sweat as she played.

By twenty-six it was over.
The bristled world brushed past her
humming with electricity
and the rooms grew silent. Pushed
in a velvet chair through slurring crowds,
she'd catch the whispered, "Isn't that . . .?"
and the "Are you sure? I thought
she was dead." The rage then, a
muck of rage at doctors,

dead-eyed parents, her own
inexcusable body. This piece
or that of music would beat at her
weeks without mercy—no way
to play it and get rid of it! Some nights
she held the cello in bed, just held it,
quiet in her arms, a man
she could no longer have.

4

The glass morning brims with light.
We drink it in. Look out
at the sky, the last sparks of snow
adrift in a bewildered blue. The
music has long since clicked
itself off, leaving silence to build
around us as around a diving bell. How
much pressure must *she* be under,
decades dead, who would sing out,
"C-sharp!" when the telephone rang?
Silence was never her métier,
and now she's up to her ears in it.

Or that's how it plays from here,
in the outer, where spirit is forced
to shoulder its way
though large wooden objects.

II

The Clutter of Was

A Face at the Window

for Henry James

New snow races east along 14th,
driving hustlers under awnings,
their shouts fading upward, mixed
with the smoke of scorched chestnuts.

Buses barge past, but sounds
the ear no longer hears stop you
in your disappearing tracks: a crackle,

yes, of firewood, and the whispers
of an absent child. Where
has he gone? Walk on, head down
like a dousing rod—not here,
not here, warmer, past the avoiding eyes
of three-card-monte players. Lean
against a bent No Parking sign
in front of 58, cut-rate appliances
in the throes of a final closeout.

Something is here that is no longer here.
No picket gate, yet you hear it creak.
A wooden porch where none has been
for a century. Snow whips by, veiling
and unveiling the scene. *There:*

a parlor window, and a boy
looking out at you. His eyes are curious,
impersonal, his brown hair
raked carelessly to the side. You know him.
Those buttons! He wore that same
tight-fitting vest for the daguerreotype.

Already he was one on whom
nothing is lost, not even
the future staring him in the face.

Correspondence

As soon as I held Mr. Hawthorne's book
I knew I must review it, and more,
must know its author.
                              Have you
never felt the jump of blood, Sir,
coming upon words only a kindred soul
could write?
                    Those were heady days.
My notice proved my note of introduction,
for he, too, I believe, felt the joy
of being understood.
                            Our friendship
changed as he grew famous, and I,
after the failure of my Whale, grew less so,
all but forgotten, though I published
book after botched book, my heart consumed
by what it fed on.
                        He was as dark as I,
but sought light, made himself
the public man you see and, I am grieved
to say, cooled to our correspondence.

I saw him too well. My letters
were an embarrassment, and I am told
he burned them. Of course he burned them.
I would have escaped me, too, if I could.

If you see him in London, Sir,
please convey my kindest compliments.

                        Yours ever, etc.,
                            Melville

Paula and Clara

The way to *this is*. Not easy to find when you know
how it ends, the clutter of *was*. Hard enough
finding one's own face in the brass
plaque of the New York Trust pulsing with taxis
in our brazen century. How much harder
to follow, in a yellowed book, Englished
from an uncongenial tongue, the thread
of an argument even the Old World has lost
interest in arguing—follow it back
through a disused labyrinth till you see
nothing in the dark save the line,
only the line before you, silver-blue as a vein
of electricity held between thumb and forefinger.

At last a funnel of trees opens to a clearing, the rise
of a country road, two women in white walking
away from you hand in hand toward the house the songs
are floating from. You recall a print in a book,
the same white manse stuck in a muck of peat bogs,
sheepfolds, birches and pines known as Worpswede,
where painters and peasants pass in silence at evening
in narrow lanes. Wind scatters guitar notes over the moor.
A party's underway, this time for a young writer
named Rilke, back from Russia, and of course
the "sisters" must come: Paula, smaller, quick-eyed,
and Clara, her lunging features framed in ringlets,
who studied last spring with Rodin.

With his narrow wrists and hungering eyes, Rilke can add
nothing to such women. From one of them, he will learn,
he can subtract, as a hand reaching toward a bell—and
      touching it—
reduces it to silence. The other will ring and ring madly
to the end: Look, she is twirling with earnest Otto Modersohn,

while Clara, in white batiste fastened in the Empire style
under the bosom, leans perfectly against an armchair.

Late that night, a light knock. Rilke crosses
to the door, and there stand the two of them, flushed
with daring. Come in! He'd refused to dance, had left,
yet they'd *come*—the tall sculptress
and her painter friend with the imperative eyes. He
pushes the window wide, and they lean out
laughing. Their foreheads pulse in the cold.

Now they grow silent, watching the moon tilt
over the poplars. Something is stirring in all of them.
In her journal Paula will write: *"I know
I shall not live very long. But I wonder,
is that sad?"* It is September, and time turns
forgetful, its purposes lost among moon-tarnished trees.
Whom does he love, this writer among artists? What
does it matter? Both. He finds himself in Paula's
studio, steam curling from their cups. They speak
of Tolstoy, death, "and what makes us feel eternal."
Her voice has folds, like silk. Her hair has moments
of gold, then dims as a shadow moves through.
It covers her hands, glides over her lap, her bodice,
her face. Behind them stand the paintings
he will not comprehend till after her death
he finds himself in an exhibition of Cézanne.
Then he will go back. Then he will look at her nude
self-portrait and try to meet the gaze that will not say,
"That's me," but simply: "This is."

A year later all are fatally married: Paula and Otto,
Clara and Rainer—brief tales that take four lives to tell.
Rilke fades from family after a two-years' try. Modersohn's
palette learns darker moods than he'd mixed before
when he sees his wife surpass him. She moves

to Paris and brightens. *"If I can paint three good pictures, then
I shall go gladly, with flowers in my hair."* He begs. She
returns. Soon she is pregnant. Giving birth, she pins
roses to her dressing gown and winds her braids in a crown.

It's a celebration, her rising from bed for the first time. Otto
has lit candles everywhere, chandelier, side tables, every surface
flagrant with joy. Paula stands and walks lightly ahead of him.
The child is brought. For a moment she holds her. Then
sudden heaviness pulls her dreadfully down—*thrombosis*,
the doctors will say. Her last words: *What a pity . . .*

Now, in America, over a hundred years on,
where memory is scratched and painted over
and scratched again, and great horn blasts announce the future,
always the future, it is a long-ago afternoon, year
1900, you return to: the day Paula and Clara got in dutch
sneaking into a locked church, climbing stone
steps to the tower and ringing the bells, the two of them
swinging up and down by the ropes, their hands burning, till,
deafened and delirious, they happen to look down and see
crowds forming . . .

Going to Ground

I seek you, Robert Lowell, but you are safe,
your brain too dense a briar, although your line,
tight, close-crammed, muscled, tense as a buck

about to make a break for it, shows more
sovereign wit than any ten technicians
in their learned lairs. Now you've gone

to ground where none of your wives can find you,
the Brahmin drawl silenced, kindness and cruelty
consigned, with your madness, to monographs.

The Deer Come Down

for Edward Weismiller

Expecting any moment an apparition
of deer, brown amid the green haze
of April woods, while the sun swoons
lower through spangled branches
and even the flare of redbud
starts to dim, I lean on the fence rail

thinking of poets we've lost, or are soon
to lose, those most alert to the turn
of a leaf, or a line, the lift
of wind or veil, the faint complaint
of elm limbs rubbing together, those
among us who sensed, without seeing,

the first of the deer descend, testing
the air, flicking their white tails.

The Rivers

for Martha Gellhorn

They crossed a narrow river. *What
river?* Martha thought. So many rivers
one crossed and did not notice—or died
without sorting it out, blue threads
in a tangle, the woman reclusive,
funny, but sharp of tongue, known
as a former wife of the big-game
writer, though her war dispatches
took better aim than his, unclouded
by ego, though ego she had, she just
got out of the way of it. What river,
in what country were there willows
along a brown stream, and washing
hung out to dry on lower branches,
and who was she, brought up
with facecreams and bubble baths,
to be there? No one knew
what to do with a blonde
in a war zone. They stamped
her papers, let her cross
the checkpoint by the river. *What river?*
she wondered, living by herself now
in Wales. The rivers ran together,
the one by the shell-shaken dive
in Barcelona, or the glum hotel
in Prague, where she charmed
barfuls of journalistic bogarts
then scooped them all. Turns out,
despite a high-end education
and Mrs. Roosevelt's ear, she got
herself out of her nice hometown
and into the swim of—what river

was it where the boys dove like frogs
and a bridge curved up slender
and high as her own high-held head
while down below three rowboats
dipped, pink and blue and yellow?

She lied her way into the storm
of D-Day, showed up at Dachau,
hating the tyrants who finally
had their own dark waters
to row. Lenin sank to death
raving of electricity; Stalin,
his left arm raised from the bed
to ward off wolves. Hitler
gobbled cream cakes in the bunker
and fingered his Luger. The old men
are gone now. Younger
have taken over, and even those who vow
never to forget cannot tell
one from another.
                    At the end,
light filtering through the curtains
of the house in Wales, she
remembered the day the bridges
were bombed, the river in flood,
while little planes droned sweetly
over the broken town. *What town?*
What river was it? she wondered,
and turned away.

The Ezra

O to be in England
       among the well-to-do

year of our Lord
       Nineteen-Aught-Nine

and be Pound—
       not the British greenback

but the Ezra,
       the jenyouine article, minted

in Idaho, his hair
       a prairie fire, loco

motives rumbling
       through his chest, his brain

bursting with Provençal,
       profanity, and, yes,

kindness. There he goes now,
       quick of step,

rounding a corner
       in Kensington.

Today he's having tea
       with the Shakespears,

"quite the nicest people
       in London . . ."

Tomorrow who knows . . .
       Tom Eliot? God?

Leave him here.
Do not prophesy.
Give him this day:

a young man in a hurry, hungry, and in love.

Visit to Rutherford

for William Eric Williams

Thanks much to Bill
who showed me
where the kettle was
and left me

alone in the house
among the Pound, Zukofsky,
and rafts
of Williams:

Paterson signed to Floss,
The Wedge, The Clouds,
The Tempers
jammed every which way,

contentious still
in the silence
and plump comforts
of the front room.

I take my notes
but know I am the one
missing, the ghost
in the house,

feeding off leavings,
off the air itself,
as if the desk
still creaked under his elbow.

Time to get clear of this,
rinse the cup,
head out back
into the blooming yard.

"Horseshit," calls Bill,
unloading heavy bags
from the car.
"The garden won't grow without it."

Early for Angels

for James Merrill

Too early? Simply there,
alone in a
round room
at the Guggenheim:

James on a wooden chair,
waiting for a
ceremony, or a com-
panionable rhyme,

legs crossed, hands
composed on his lap,
happy to serve
whatever sublime

tribunal calls him.
He is early for angels,
but his heart
is out of time.

Miss Subways

for Lawrence Ferlinghetti

"Meet Miss Subways," you wrote
the year my father
dragged a final breath
through the silent room.

I never met Miss Subways.
I was too busy
whispering, "Come *on*,
Dad, one more!" too busy being
fourteen, too busy carrying
a hole the size of Utah
in my skinny chest.

Then came the scattering
of ashes at Jones Beach,
and I was too busy
throwing gritty stuff
into the waves
against a stinging wind

to meet Miss Subways
riding the Times Square
Shuttle back and forth
at four in the morning, like you,
Larry, and your hipster pals
who were with it
when I was without.

Yet the day would come,
whether in time hip, or
in time square, when I would ride
those same racketing cars
all night with your poems

in my pocket, and on my knee
a trembling notebook
filled with unspeakable words
as I tunneled the dark,
searching for Miss Subways.

Pouring the Wine

for Agha Shahid Ali

Light slashes through pines into the world.
Cities lift their spines into the world.

All things are echoes. A line becomes the Nile.
The Nile bears all that shines into the world.

Bear down, dig in, delve into love's defile.
Pull the ore from mines into the world.

You are my voice, my eyes, my feet, my hands.
Inject my anodynes into the world.

The water reddens. Drink, my changing friend.
Pour the mystic wines into the world.

The Territory

for Ralph Ellison

1. 1961

Night was a live current
outside the boxcar door
the week I fled,

a torn teen
hitching south, hoping to reach
a territory

of my own. Rain
was the only constant,
my throat raw

with longing, for what,
dear God? On my return
I blurted my tale,

and he strode
across the crew-cut campus
telling his own boxcar story,

hilarious, of heading east
to college. "But officer!"
he'd said as detectives

brandishing nickel-plated
.45s rousted him
from the train, "I'm a student!"

By then it was a joke he told,
ending in a gutty laugh,
leaving out everything.

Long after, I found the photo
Tuskegee took
of arriving students: Ellison, comma,

Ralph, white gauze taped
to his forehead, a gash
by the temple,

and his not-there eyes.

2. 1988

Eight floors over Harlem
and not far from eighty, he fingers

a wet cigar. Still visible
and still not, an old Quixote

tilting against the man
in the mirror.

"The future American,"
he says, "will hide, even

as he shows himself."
Another turn of the cigar.

He stares out over the Hudson.
"A trickster," he says, laughter

rumbling up, eyes hooded, skull
balding to stone. In the next room

a manuscript squats.
We do not speak of it.

Below, the river uncoils,
glittering like mica.

The Great War

for Paul Fussell

1983

"You know," he said, walking us
to the midnight bus, "it will all
end badly." We tried to jolly him
out of it, but no go. This

after a fine evening at his new
divorcé digs. Not the manse
on Lilac Lane, where favored grads
cavorted after finals, just

a pad on the main drag, but still
Princeton, and he its oddly
genial curmudgeon, eyes narrowed
on some distant aperçu, his voice
testing it into an epigram

on human devilment. *Nihil
admirari* was the text on which
his books were sermons.

Earlier, at the flat, he smoked
the place up with swordfish, regaled us
with plans and a happy Chablis,
and signed *The Great War
and Modern Memory* with love.

2010

Dr. Johnson, sage, solid
as the stone he kicked
to refute a bishop, lived
like all of us in fear

of losing balance. Berryman
tumbled off a bridge. Plath
ducked in an oven. Pound,

unsteady for decades, declared
at the end, "I wasn't mad,
I was a moron."

"It will all end badly."
Paul's way of putting it. Fluid
in the brain threw
his balance to hell. The shunt

didn't help. Now, not mad,
not writing, doing well
for eighty-six, he stumps about
with a cane, reads his own books,

declaring, "I have stopped learning
and begun remembering."

Moonrise at Ashcroft

Silver crashed and the lights went out in Ashcroft.
A century passes in a dream.
Some houses stand,

some sink in cellar holes. Gooseberry bushes
planted by pie-loving prospectors
mark where they stood,

tufts in the clefts of fields. Only night
is the same, the arguing stream
shadowed by the same

humped mountain. This is what Jack Leahy,
the town's ghost-poet, heard
from the stump on his porch

while he waited for moonrise: the cuffing breeze,
the ceaseless moil of water, hushing
and shouting at once.

This is the hour. The wind dies. The mountain's
shoulder glows. A shadow
begins its retreat

down Main Street like a coverlet slipping
from a bed. Now sudden
brightness flares

over the peak, glazing the meadow, the leaves
of a hundred thousand aspens
on the opposite slope, the roof

of the Hotel View and blacksmith's shop.
Click off the flashlight. Write
on the silver page.

Madman Attacks Statue

Whack of an axe in the backyard.
Little Billy, 2, reacts: laughs
and laughs! At 30, Bill Williams
laughs again, this time at the sight
of beauty's throat (as he sees it)
slit before his eyes at the New
York Armory show. Listen my
townspeople (whack!) I must tell you
(whack!) so much depends upon (whack!)
the laughter of astonishment.

My way was otherwise. Age 2,
at the smack of sun on snow, I
set my cap up Beverly Road.
Mommy scrambled after, scooped me
in her arms, carried me back. Off
I went again, up the great hill,
was brought back, laughing, and back, but
my course was set. In time the snow
saddened and sank in whiskered yards
and tar warmed the paving stones. But
always the straight line, and always
the round town by the bay rose up
as high as the world and brown
as morning bread and held me home.

And when, at 30, with the world's
cities in my eyes, I saw the face
of beauty cracked by a mad
man's hammer, I set off at once
down dizzying pages, to save
and to repair, although I knew
no human pen could put the
Pietà back together again.

III

Crossing Against the Light

The Silk Dress

You have been going down
dawdling when suddenly she
sweeps up the staircase,

loose hair streaming, her dress
an avalanche of lost
messages. Turn

on your heel. After her.
In a moment reverse
a lifetime of error.

Rue des Halles

It is a see-through day, Parisian sun
burning through mist, women in summer white
(from where I sit sipping *une bière pression*)
suddenly nude as they cross against the light.

Hours I searched for the lewd house where I lost
what claim I had to innocence a score
of lives ago. Now in its place this bistro,
farting motorbikes, and tourists galore.

Which doesn't explain the girl sipping wine
two tables away, one foot up on a chair,
or why a boy's heart wildly beats in mine
to see her white neck, and arms long and bare.

The Red Blouse

Across Kansas on cruise control
he drives toward a woman's body.
Stubbled fields flush orange

in the final light. He squeezes
the pedal . . . 75 . . . 80,
a mad organist playing his deepest note.

Ahead 200 miles, a woman
crosses a room, sweetens
her tea, meets with students. But

something's off. A humming
like bees, like tires over darkening roads,
patrols her mind.

She searches the mirror for clues.
A coil of hair, loosened, hangs
like a bellpull. She pins it up. No

use. Nothing is any use.
She touches her breast lightly
through the red blouse.

Sharing the Mirror

I move through darkness to the light's first ache
and clamber down the stations of the womb.
A bridge dissolves behind me, and I wake.

I learn that there are other dawns to break,
and while a mother sings, *Aloo, Aloom,*
I move through darkness to the light's first ache.

Through leaves I watch them swimming in the lake,
their thin laughter a maddening perfume.
A bridge dissolves behind me, and I wake.

My father, in what's surely a mistake,
is coughing blood. I feel a greening doom
and move through darkness to the light's first ache.

Alone with words, I'm learning what's at stake,
and how, with love, words rub, hum, warm, and bloom.
A bridge dissolves behind me, and I wake.

Now our eyes meet in a rich double-take,
and share the mirror in a secret room.
We move through darkness to the light's first ache.
A bridge dissolves behind us, and we wake.

Star Cemetery

By snow-brushed fields we drove
the little red rental
deeper through Kansas, our
baby in your belly,
wipers slapping aside
wet flakes. We passed a house,
a light on in the parlor,
a pickup parked out back,
then nothing, a red-tailed hawk
coming in low, more trees,
and the old wooden sign
to Star Cemetery.

To this last, lost place, plot
bought and paid for in sight
of field and God and your
shy ancestors, we came
with no clear reason but
to kiss, to say, *This is our
secret*. But the kiss smeared
the winter sky, and cold
hands found warm prey in a
flurry of buttons. That day
our covenant was sealed
at the edge of the rocking grave.

The Changing Table

for Grace

At first, neat and white
as a winter field, it is far

too big for you.
A few

months later you lie
at an angle to fit at all,

dangling one heel
over the rail like some giggling

Gulliver. Who would suppose
you'd outgrow the place

you came to be changed?
You look up at me

as I snap your clothes, and your eyes
are cities.

The Spy

Outside looking in, the sun
in decline behind me,
I spy on my wife.

She sits at the table.
Her body bends
over a page.

She does not see
the shiver of gold
in her chestnut hair

or suspect the stare
of my reflected eyes. *See me,*
I silently command.

She does not turn.
The window's crosses rise
in the cooling air.

See me, I whisper
to the phantom
in the empty chair.

The Hands

Head stuffed, ears
stopped, eyes

deceived. Yes,
but the hands, palms

buzzing with news,
have done

rough work, stacked
wood,

stroked the head
of a child, washed

each other
like best friends.

Look at them, lined
with zodiacs.

They burn
like metal detectors. Close

your eyes. Listen
to no one. Think

of nothing.
Hold out your hands.

An Arrangement of Hearts

Thinking about kings
and how to keep
from winning

I fail to notice
her head lower
over the cards.

An arrangement
of hearts
tips forward. "Mom,"

I say, knowing she'd
want to play it out,
"Mom, it's your move."

Death scene in stained bathrobe?
Her hair red
as a setter, white

shining through. But look:
the blue eyes
open wide:

"Are you sure, dear?
Oh!" (Smiling.)
"I seem to have gin!"

Wave

A trick of October light
made festive the trek we
took to the empty beach,

the four of us (five
counting the box
tucked in the knapsack).

You to thank, Mother,
for my bare feet in the sand,
brother beside me, our wives

to the right, the sea's
blue cylinders rolling up,
rolling slowly away.

We fought open the lid,
looked at each other,
and waded in, two brothers

for once shoulder to shoulder
in an enterprise. He
dug in first, flung fistfuls

into the wind, flecks of
crushed bone sinking at once,
finer granules riding

in little cloud puffs, as if
from a last cigarette.
Then I joined in, gripped

by a wild, grieving joy,
till the thing was done. I let
receding water run

through my numb fingers,
and stared out: blue, blue.
Lovely to turn, then,

and see the women
waiting on higher ground,
windblown and waving us home.

In the Grand Hotel

The Grand Hotel: always the same. People
come. People go. Nothing ever happens. Well,

I did meet Garbo in her satin suite
and scribbled on her breast. A villanelle

it was, not my best, but with her giggling
it's lucky I did better than doggerel. Oh

yes, I lost a fortune, and yelled at my boss,
all before the ding of the dinner bell.

And then, of course, I died. Mustn't leave
that out. An old ploy, but it ends well.

The lout who brained me with a telephone
was soon whisked to a dirty cell.

Sending the old boy off in cuffs made it
almost all right for me to head for hell,

at least till I remembered: I was he,
and he, and she the lovely demoiselle,

even my own dog, who misses me
as I miss me. I'm the suspicious smell

behind the closet door, the crumpled note
thrown on the floor, a spill of muscatel.

Listen. The music has stopped. It is so quiet.
It has never been so quiet in the Grand Hotel.

Heliopause

For my final dream
I'll conjure an afternoon on a windy rise
at the mouth of the Bío-bío and the line
where river bled

into sea, the sweet
collision of it, waves helmeted
in white, though there are wilder realms
even than these

along the border
of interstellar night, where solar gusts
expire and gaseous stars
no longer lift

the hair on the nape.
Out there, at the edge of the sun's lost influence,
I'll stand, with all the known behind me, and all
heaven ahead.

Notes on the poems:

"A Minor God." German composer Ferdinand Hiller (1811–1885) was a piano prodigy. At age 15 he was brought to meet the dying Beethoven.

"The Return." Clair Leonard (1901–1963) was a gentle soul who chaired the Music Department at Bard College (NY) for many years.

"Requiem." Blind jazz pianist Lennie Tristano (1919-1978) was one of the most innovative musicians of his time. I heard of his death during my year teaching in southern Chile.

"A Face at the Window." Henry James (1843–1916) spent several childhood years at 58 West 14th Street in New York City.

"Paula and Clara." Paula Becker (1876–1907), painter and close friend of Rilke's, married fellow painter Otto Modersohn. She died at age 31, after giving birth to her first child. Clara Westhoff (1878-1954), married Rilke in 1901 and bore him a daughter, Ruth.

"The Rivers." Martha Gellhorn (1908–1998) was a fiercely intelligent novelist and journalist. For several years she was also the third wife of Ernest Hemingway.

"Early for Angels." The death of poet James Merrill (1926–1995), a magical man, hit the literary world particularly hard.

"Pouring the Wine." Born in New Delhi and raised in Kashmir, Agha Shahid Ali (1949–2001) published seven volumes of poetry in English. He was a champion of the ghazal, and his enthusiasm and sweet nature made him a beloved figure among fellow poets.

Acknowledgments

Magazines

Bardian:	"The Return"
I-70 Review:	"Visit to Rutherford," "The Spy," "Going to Ground," "In the Grand Hotel"
The Journal:	"An Arrangement of Hearts"
New Letters:	"The Changing Table," "The Rivers"
North American Review:	"Star Cemetery," "The Territory," "A Face at the Window"
nthWORD:	"The Great War"
The Paris Review:	"Moonrise at Ashcroft," "Paula and Clara," "Wave"
phoebe:	"Madman Attacks Statue"
Western Humanities Review:	"The Cellist," "Mozart's Pigtail," "Sharing the Mirror"
The Yale Review:	"The Red Blouse," "Heliopause"

Anthologies

JM: A Remembrance, edited by Robin and Mark Magowan. New York: The Academy of American Poets, 1996: "Early for Angels"

Poetry: An Introduction (fourth edition), edited by Michael Meyer. Boston and New York: Bedford/St. Martin's, 2004: "The Red Blouse"

Poets at Large, edited by H.L. Hix. Kansas City: Helicon Nine Editions, 1997: "The Hands," "Rue des Halles"

Ravishing DisUnities, edited by Agha Shahid Ali. Hanover and London: Wesleyan University Press, 2000: "Pouring the Wine"

The Whirlybird Anthology of Kansas City Writers, edited by Vernon Rowe, Maryfrances Wagner, David Ray, and Judy Ray. Shawnee, KS: Whirlybird Press, 2012: "The Deer Come Down," "Miss Subways," "Rue des Halles"

About the Author

Mozart's Pigtail is Roderick Townley's third full collection of poetry. He has published books in several other genres and received a number of honors, among them the Governor's Arts Award, the Peregrine Prize for Short Fiction, a Master Artist Fellowship in Fiction, the Thorpe Menn Award, three Kansas Notable Book awards, and two prizes from the Academy of American Poets.

His children's novels have appeared in several foreign editions, as well as in large print, audio, and book-club versions. One of them, *The Blue Shoe* (Knopf), was illustrated by Harry Potter artist Mary GrandPré. Another, *The Great Good Thing* (Atheneum), has been optioned for film and made into an opera.

After earning his PhD at Rutgers, Roderick taught in Chile on a Fulbright Fellowship and worked in New York as a journalist and editor before moving to Kansas with his wife, Poet Laureate of Kansas Emerita Wyatt Townley.

www.rodericktownley.com

BkMk Press is grateful for the support it has recently received
from the following organizations and individuals:

Missouri Arts Council
Miller-Mellor Foundation
Neptune Foundation
Richard J. Stern Foundation for the Arts
Stanley H. Durwood Foundation
William T. Kemper Foundation

Beverly Burch
Jaimee Wriston Colbert
Maija Rhee Devine
Whitney and Mariella Kerr
Carla Klausner
Lorraine M. López
Patricia Cleary Miller
Margot Patterson
Alan Proctor
James Hugo Rifenbark
Roderick and Wyatt Townley

CPSIA information can be obtained
at www.ICGtesting.com
Printed in the USA
FSHW010738061020